Cana Academy® Guide

LEADING A DISCUSSION ON THE U.S. CONSTITUTION

Mary Frances Loughran

PUBLISHED BY

CANA ACADEMY®
www.canaacademy.org

© 2018 Cana Academy®

THE UNITED STATES CONSTITUTION
Grades 9-12
Recommended hours: 25 (including lecture time)

INTRODUCTION

The Declaration of Independence, the Constitution, and the Bill of Rights form the foundation of American government. Every American citizen should possess at least a rudimentary understanding of these texts, and it is important for students to study them within their historical context. This context provides the essential background necessary for understanding the utterly unique character of the American Constitution.

American constitutionalism has philosophical, religious and practical roots. It was built on tradition and custom as well as experience and study. Many constitutional issues are controversial, and debates over interpretation abound. The Framers themselves had significant disagreements, and students should understand that the final product was the result of a great deal of discussion and compromise. Although this guide does not address every possible argument or cover every relevant source upon which the Framers relied, it does provide some basic background information to orient the students to a careful reading of the Constitution.

The teacher will need to decide how much of the information included here is appropriate for the students. We recommend an introductory lecture using the information provided here as a guide. While the students may not benefit from a lengthier discussion of the thornier issues or a study of the multitude of sources that informed the Framers, the teacher should be as well-versed as possible and thereby able to respond to questions the students may raise as they begin their reading of the Constitution. We recommend the excellent sources in the bibliography for the teacher's further study.

Furthermore, prior to this unit, we encourage teachers to address the principles embodied in the Declaration of Independence (see the Cana Academy Guide, *Leading a Discussion on the Declaration of Independence*) and to cover the major events leading up to the War for Independence (see Appendix C for a list of events). The PBS series *Liberty* provides an overview of the war. William Bennett's *Last Best Hope, Volume I* provides a good narrative for the students.

The following are included in this guide:

- Historical context leading to the 1787 Grand Convention at Philadelphia (i.e., the Constitutional Convention)

- Philosophical ideas shared by members of the Grand Convention

- A treatment of the main issues that raised obstacles to ratification: the disagreements between the Federalists and the Anti-Federalists; the debates over mixed government; the disagreements over slavery; the concerns over the absence of a bill of specific, individual rights

- A brief remark on the importance of the religious commitments of the Founders

- Discussion questions to lead students through the Preamble to the Constitution and the Constitution itself

- Discussion questions and possible corresponding responses for the Bill of Rights

- Broader questions suitable for essay assignments or further discussion

- Appendices: a list of online resources; a list of relevant documents that could be read by students; a list of important events leading to the drafting of the Constitution; and interesting facts surrounding the founding

- A bibliography for teachers

HISTORICAL CONTEXT OF THE GRAND CONVENTION OF 1787

With the adoption of the Declaration of Independence at the Second Continental Congress (1776), the colonies had not only declared their independence from Great Britain but had declared the right to "[a]dopt such a government as shall, in the opinion of the representatives of the people, best conduce to the safety and happiness of their constituents and America in general." It was Thomas Paine's *Common Sense* that had provided the reassurance needed for support of a declaration of independence. The idea that effective government could be provided by self-governing Americans had been a stumbling block until Paine convincingly and entirely dismissed the British constitution for its dependence upon monarchy. In the years prior to, during, and after the war, each state wrote and ratified its own constitution. Similarities between the states' constitutions are evidence that the principles later embodied in the Constitution of the United States were widely discussed and, in many cases, widely accepted. At the war's conclusion and as each colony ratified its own constitution, thirteen separate and independent states emerged.

Each state constitution professes the love of liberty that had been the catalyst for independence. Liberty, long established in English law and tradition, had been articulated as consent of the governed in the Declaration of Independence. Jefferson drew upon not only these British traditions but also the state constitutions, particularly George Mason's Declaration of Rights penned in 1776.

Also important to these colonists was the rule of law—a tradition inherited from Britain's long, unique, and often bloody fight for freedom from arbitrary power. In fact, it was precisely the violation of the rule of law by Britain (e.g. the Declaratory Act) that propelled the colonies toward liberation from what had become a tyranny.

Strong, centralized governance that threatened representative legislatures was rejected in most state constitutions with each expressing a firm belief in the capacity of power to corrupt at all levels of government. Even representative government as provided for by Parliament had proven to be susceptible to corruption. Parliament had stood as the vanguard since 1689, protecting British citizens from corrupt hereditary monarchies. But the monarchy was only checked by Parliament, not eliminated. Parliament represented the two social classes—commons and lords—all subjects of the king. It seems clear that while colonists had considered themselves British subjects represented by Parliament, it was never the case, due to distance and differences, that this representation would be total. Each colony was established by a charter—some royal, some commercial—but by the time war was ignited, the colonies had turned away from Parliament and towards the king as members of an empire united by its monarch. As royal colonies, it was the king who was responsible for the interests of the colonies. With Parliament threatening the economic freedom of the colonies, it was increasingly believed that the king should protect those interests. He failed to do so, ignoring their pleas and showing approval of Parliament's unlawful actions.

Unifying these states to wage a war against an empire proved to be one of the most difficult tasks facing the Continental Congress. The meeting at Philadelphia of delegates from each of the states lacked unity; consequently, the requisition of funds and soldiers from the states was unenforceable. The Second Continental Congress, during the years 1775 through 1777, penned several versions of the Articles of Confederation, settling on a final version for submission to the states in 1777. The Articles established a loose structure under which it was hoped that states could be compelled to send money and men to support the war effort. By 1779, only Maryland remained a hold-out finally ratifying the Articles in March of 1781.

However, the weakness of a centralized government, whose authority reached to the states rather than the individual citizens of each state, confirmed that such requests would remain unenforceable. How does a government force a state to do anything except by fines or war, neither of which were acceptable options? Because the Articles did not create a union of the states and did not establish separate branches of government, they did not provide what Hamilton described as the "energetic executive" necessary for requisitioning men and money, the necessities for which the Articles were formulated in the first place.

The Articles of Confederation established a truly federal, not national government, an alliance of sovereign and independent states. With many members of Congress suspicious of any attempt to establish a national government, representatives labored under the loose Articles of Confederation for several years. It should be noted that Americans successfully concluded the war with Britain, secured an alliance to do so, and created a treaty with Great Britain, all under the auspices of this loose confederation. However, border and trade disputes that had disrupted order, even while at war with Britain, threatened their ambitions for liberty and only grew in frequency after the war's conclusion. Furthermore, there was reason to believe that because the newly independent states were not fully recovered from war, the French, the

Spanish or even Great Britain again would attempt to assert control over them. In fact, Great Britain had not yet withdrawn from the states according to the provisions of the 1783 Treaty of Paris.

Through an exchange of letters, George Washington and James Madison expressed concern that the states, having won independence, would not enjoy peaceful commercial trade without a national government. The unity required to win war against the greatest military on earth was slowly eroded as the factious states engaged in border and trade disputes. The precious liberty paid for by years of war was now threatened by a level of disunity that made the states powerless against aggressive European powers. In fact, many in Europe believed that time would prove the colonies incapable of self-government—the heart of the Declaration of Independence.

All attempts to modify the Articles had failed. Many of the political and military players of the war now increasingly saw the necessity of turning their attention to consideration of a national government, one free of the disabilities of the Articles of Confederation. Thus, in September 1786, Madison and the Virginia legislature convened a meeting of all the states' representatives in Annapolis, Maryland. There, it was agreed that a Grand Convention would be held the following May (1787) in Philadelphia. The publicly stated purpose of the convention was to revise the Articles of Confederation. It was not agreed that the Articles would be abandoned and a new national constitution written. Thus, this meeting was called the Grand Convention by those who attended, not the Constitutional Convention.

Fifty-five delegates gathered from all the states except Rhode Island. Of those in attendance, thirty-nine signed the final, proposed Constitution to be taken back to the states for debate and ratification. Article VII calls for ratification by nine states before adoption. This constitution, though written by a handful of their representatives, would be voted upon through assembly of the citizens of the states, making it the Constitution of the United States on June 21, 1788, the first truly democratic institution of government in history.

Before beginning a study of the Constitution, some details about the convention and the participants help the students grasp the unprecedented nature of this historic event. The teacher may take advantage of the websites and books listed in the appendix and bibliography.

Depending on the age of the students and how much time is allotted for this study, teachers may want to include additional material. We think this guide represents the minimum that any educated adult should know about the Constitution. One good introduction to this study is to have students take an online citizenship test and discuss what they know about the Constitution before beginning their formal study (see Appendix A: Online Sources). We recommend *The Heritage Guide to the Constitution* as an excellent resource for further research and information. Teachers should have a copy to use as an aid to their own understanding.

PHILOSOPHICAL IDEAS SHARED BY THE GRAND CONVENTION

Teachers may want to begin with a discussion of government in general: What is it? How is government different from other kinds of associations, e.g., families? What is its purpose? it pose a threat to liberty? Defining some terms from the start is helpful for the students. The following definitions provide a foundational understanding of the concepts informing the delegates gathered in Philadelphia. We encourage teachers to pose questions to the students for discussion in order to cover this material in a seminar rather than a lecture format.

Liberty, as understood by the Founders, refers to a network of rights and responsibilities. Although many had read and agreed with Locke on consent of the governed, many of the men in attendance rejected his understanding of government as a social contract. As James Otis had earlier argued, "Government is therefore most evidently founded on the necessities of our nature. It is by no means an arbitrary thing depending merely on compact or human will for its existence" (as quoted in Beitzinger, 121). Believing that man is by nature social and that the isolated human being living outside of any community is a fiction, they rejected the notion that government is simply a necessary evil. Informed by various theological and religious commitments, each believed that man's nature was to some degree corrupted; to protect liberty, governments must be instituted. But government does not magically transform nature; thus, it too must be guarded against, lest it threaten individual liberty. As Samuel Adams stated, "… the true patriot will constantly be jealous of those very men, knowing that power, especially in times of corruption, makes men wanton, that it intoxicates the mind; and unless those with whom it is entrusted are carefully watched—such is the weakness or perverseness of human nature—they will be left to domineer over the people, instead of governing them according to the known laws of the state, to which alone they have submitted" (as quoted in Beitzinger 140-141).

Thus, the reasonable community sets limits and establishes responsibilities for the fullest expression of liberty. None of the Framers believed that liberty was license, and, to some degree, all believed that human flourishing lay in the exercise of ordered liberty: that is, liberty subject to either reason or a higher law or both. They believed that man has an end, and, because he can know his end, he is obligated to act towards this end employing his liberty and reason. Governments are established to protect this essential human capacity.

Equality stems from our shared nature as human beings. Because of our shared nature, we further possess shared rights based upon that nature. It is important for students to understand that for the Founders this shared nature is unchanging. *Equal rights,* listed in the Declaration of Independence as the rights to life, liberty, and happiness, flow from our natural equality.

However, students should understand that not all the Framers would have agreed to this understanding of equality. Those with a Puritan or Calvinist background disagreed that all are equal, although they affirmed the *dignity* of each individual. By the late 1700s, Puritans and Calvinists could agree that all are equal under the law even if not naturally equal. It is the dignity and sovereignty, if not natural equality, that form the foundation for the primary principle of limited government: consent of the governed.

For all those in attendance, guarantees of equal outcomes were not grounded in nature and did not fall under any definition of equality.

Natural rights are not the same thing as *wants*; the desire for something does not automatically guarantee the natural right to that object of desire. Furthermore, the Founders based natural rights on unchangeable human nature, not upon grants of power from a governing body. While government may grant *civil liberties,* the Founders believed those liberties should be grounded in natural rights. Which rights are civil liberties and which are natural rights is the subject of much debate, and younger students need not delve too deeply into that debate. However, it is important that all students understand that the Founders' concept of natural rights does not create an unlimited freedom to do or have whatever one desires.

Consent of the governed played a fundamental role in the issues that led to war with Britain. The colonies inherited from Britain this hard-won tradition, but their unique circumstances transformed the expression of consent. While in Britain consent of citizens was expressed by representatives in Parliament, colonists had from the very start elected their own legislative assemblies that represented much smaller constituencies. In other words, they had established local governance. Parliament in Britain did not represent the colonists since no colonist participated in Parliament.

Therefore, it was the sovereignty of the people that was at the heart of colonial complaints.

Bernard Bailyn summarizes these issues in *Ideological Origins of the American Revolution* this way:

> On such fundamental issues—representation and consent, the nature of constitutions and of rights, the meaning of sovereignty—and in such basic ways, did the colonists probe and alter their inheritance of thought concerning liberty and its preservation. To conceive of legislative assemblies as mirrors of society and their voices as mechanically exact expressions of the people; to assume and to act upon the assumption, that human rights exist above the law and stand as the measure of the law's validity; to understand constitutions to be ideal designs of government, and fixed, limiting definitions of its permissible sphere of action, and to consider the possibility that absolute sovereignty in government need not be a monopoly of a single all-engrossing agency but the shared possession of several agencies each limited by the boundaries of the others but all-powerful within its own—to think in these ways, as Americans were doing before Independence, was to reconceive the fundamentals of government and of society's relation to government (Bailyn, *Ideological Origins,* 230).

This constitution is an expression of consent and, as such, tests the possibility of self-government. Consent need not be unanimous, and, while determinations must be arrived at by majorities, the rights of the minority are to be equally respected if self-government is to survive.

Republican government is representative government. The Framers all agreed that history showed direct democracy to be unstable and prone to violent upheavals. On the other hand, monarchies often led to tyranny; even with the parliamentary check of Great Britain's constitution, the rights of the colonists had been trampled upon.

The Framers sought to avoid the excesses of both monarchy and democracy by dividing power in a federal and republican government. Citizens would be represented by those they had chosen at both the state and national levels. Power would be further divided into three branches of government with the Senate and House loosely following Montesquieu's recommendations for Parliament. Because society was not divided into classes, the situation in America called for something different. The two houses of Congress would be based on different qualifications, different term limits, different methods of election, and different powers and responsibilities. Each member of each house was to represent his constituents while filtering popular opinion toward the common good. (See *Federalist #10* for Madison's discussion of republican government and faction.)

Constitution in this case should be understood as a limiting document. In the Constitution of the United States, written restrictions on what the intended government may do are made explicit. Local and federal authorities do not have rights; people have rights. Governments have powers granted to them through *consent of the governed.* It was their mistrust of power that led the Founders to separate and balance power. From Montesquieu, the Framers learned that separate branches of government with different responsibilities, a bicameral legislative branch, and checks and balances, could prevent the consolidation of power that poses a direct threat to liberty. These institutional means would "canalize the ubiquitous lust for power in men" (Beitzinger 63).

ISSUES ADDRESSED AT THE GRAND CONVENTION: FEDERALISTS VS. ANTI-FEDERALISTS

At the gathering in Philadelphia, there were voiced as many beliefs and opinions as there were men. Each brought to the discussion his extensive reading, his religious convictions, his knowledge of history, and his experience as a leader. Some political historians identify as many as six different "parties," characterized by nuanced differences in fundamental commitments and practical experience. Students need not know all of these differences, but the teacher will want to help them understand the differences between those who supported the adoption of the Constitution and those who did not: the Federalists (or Nationalists as they were originally called) and the Anti-Federalists.

Not everyone attending the Grand Convention saw a need for a national government; some were quite content to reach some agreed upon revision of the Articles of Confederation. Some left the convention as soon as it became clear that discussion was underway to write a national constitution. It is instructive for students to understand that, while debate and compromise were part of our governing process from the beginning, some at the convention would leave and others refuse to sign the final document.

It is instructive for students to understand the fundamental objections of the unfortunately and confusingly named Anti-Federalists. Discussion of these concerns prior to a study of the Constitution provides students with the opportunity to evaluate whether the Constitution addresses their concerns.

The terms Federalist and Anti-Federalist are confusing. The Federalists were actually those who had advocated for a national government at the convention. However, early in the ratification debates, these champions of the Constitution adopted the title Federalist, even though it is a title more appropriate to those who then, by default, were called the Anti-Federalists. The Anti-Federalists did not, in fact, oppose federalism, but because they opposed those who called themselves the Federalists, these advocates of reserved powers for the states were nevertheless deemed opponents of federalism. In other words, students need to be careful of relying on the nomenclature to distinguish between these two main factions.

The Anti-Federalists—George Mason, Patrick Henry, Richard H. Lee, George Clinton, Robert Yates, Eldridge Gerry, and Luther Martin among others—represented the leanings of those across the economic spectrum but claimed a majority share of the "middling sort." Teachers should note for students that the differences between the two parties were less over substance than over the means for attaining shared ends (Beitzinger 214).

The following is an abbreviated list of Anti-Federalist objections:

1. Truly republican governments are not capable of governing such large expanses as the states at the time included. Furthermore, states are better representatives of their citizens than a distant national government. As the states expanded, their geographical holdings would require an energetic government that would inevitably become tyrannical.

2. Representation as outlined in the Constitution is inadequate; each representative in Congress is responsible for representing the views of too many constituents and will be unable to truly represent the will of the people. During the convention, some Anti-Federalists argued for a one house legislature as a truly federal element; others argued for more representation through a bicameral legislature.

3. A bill of rights was not included or guaranteed in the document as it was sent to the states for ratification. Anti-Federalists, ever concerned first and foremost for the cause of individual liberty, believed that protections against a powerful national government were essential for the protection of liberty.

4. The unlimited power of the federal government to tax is, potentially, the unlimited power to destroy and will subvert each state's ability to tax its citizens for needs closer to home.

5. An unlimited power to raise and support an army is liable to abuse and dangerous.

6. The "necessary and proper" and "supremacy" clauses are too vague and will lead to the unassailable power of the government. Energetic government, they claimed, is by nature tyrannical. Long terms of office with no limits would contribute to a bureaucratic federal government with an interest in maintaining its own power and authority.

Students will have the opportunity to discuss the Federalist response to these objections if they read the *Federalist Papers*. For now, it is sufficient for them to be aware of the sentiments expressed at the Convention.

Despite these disagreements, all delegates to the convention shared a fear of unchecked power. Most if not all the delegates possessed a clear-eyed understanding that power at all levels is susceptible to corruption. The question for all sides in the debate was how to best protect individual citizens from that corruption, whether occurring at the state or national level. Bernard Bailyn again:

> [F]aith ran high that a better world than any that had ever been known could be built, where authority was distrusted and held in constant scrutiny; where the status of men flowed from their achievements and from their personal qualities, not from distinctions ascribed to them at birth; and where the use of power over the lives of men was jealously guarded and severely restricted. It was only where there was this defiance, this refusal to truckle, this distrust of all authority, political or social, that institutions would express human aspiration, not crush them (319).

No wonder, then, that in the initial discussions of the New Jersey and Virginia Plans, the latter was deemed suspicious. The Virginia plan had entirely scratched the Articles, something for which many delegates were completely unprepared, and put in its place a strong central government. Madison had planned for this convention, arriving early and prepared to make the argument for an entirely unique experiment in government. And it was the Virginia Plan, after crucial debate, amendment, and adoption of a *mixed government,* that eventually carried the day.

Students should understand that the Constitution establishes a *federal* system for the nation with each state retaining its own constitution. What the Convention settled upon was the creation of a constitution that would be the law of the land extending authority over the *citizens* of each state, while allowing states to retain their own specific governance. Students find it helpful to see an outline of government offices moving from city and town government up to national offices. This helps them to see the federal nature of our constitutional system.

The differences between Federalist and Anti-Federalists showed up again during debates over the "necessary and proper" and "supremacy" clauses. The disagreement over these matters was so sharp that it threatened to dissolve the Convention entirely.

Each state delegation brought to the Convention the sentiments of those they represented, and differences regarding centralized authority and representative government emerged early and were passionately expressed. Thus, even at this early stage, deep political divisions that would shape decisions in the years ahead were ardently articulated and debated.

In the end, the Constitution incorporates both federal and anti-federal principles. Students should be encouraged to think about how each party is represented in the final document. If the students need some help, the following summarizes the major accommodations for both sides:

©2018 Cana Academy®

Nationalist Elements	Anti-Federalist Elements
Representation by population in House	Equal representation in the Senate
Supremacy Clause	States retain sovereignty
Necessary & Proper Clause	Enumerated powers

ISSUES ADDRESSED AT THE GRAND CONVENTION: MIXED GOVERNMENT

Sovereignty was the fundamental issue over which the war was fought. In the colonies, it was not clear who held the sovereign power. Under the British constitution and out of the mixed government of king, commons, and nobility, Parliament had emerged as the sovereign power representing consent of the governed. The colonists, however, were not represented in Parliament; neither did a mixed government exist in the colonies.

Mixed government in the Constitution would take a new form, a form that recognized that sovereign power need not be held by one group—that, in fact, sovereignty is divisible. Montesquieu and European models, particularly Britain's unwritten constitution, express mixed government as providing representation for different societal classes. The colonies (subsequently states) did not have the cultural experience of classes: society in the colonies was not rigidly divided between the landed aristocracy, wealthy merchants and less wealthy farmers and tradesmen. So, while the Framers recognized the importance of *mixed government* for its ability to provide a diversity of opinion on political matters, the categories to be mixed were unclear.

The ingenious suggestion initiated by Roger Sherman and reintroduced by Oliver Ellsworth, known as the Connecticut Compromise, solved the first hurdle of the convention: By providing a bicameral legislature with different qualifications, terms, and duties, the interests of all citizens would be represented. This would be the form that *mixed government* would assume in these new states. In addition, this further separation of power divided sovereignty, thus preventing the tyranny of any one power.

The Federalists maintained throughout that it is the people who are sovereign, not the states, and just governments derive their authority from the people. The Anti-Federalists wanted representation of the people but believed the states were best positioned for that representation. Both sides, however, recognized that the people are not immune to corruption; direct democracy becomes the tyrannical rule of the majority. The Founders, therefore, established a *republican* form of government that would act as a filter or funnel for diverse opinions to come together toward a common good and through the agency of representatives. How many representatives in total and how many from each state thus became crucial elements of the plan. Heated debate over proportional representation vs. equal representation was the order of the day until a bicameral legislative body with different qualifications for representation was reintroduced—the compromise that prevented the threatening dissolution of the Convention.

With power divided by both a federal system, a national government of three branches, and a bicameral legislature, the Framers established a system that divided sovereignty through mixed government and planted it firmly in consent of the governed.

ISSUES ADDRESSED AT THE GRAND CONVENTION: SLAVERY

In addition to the debate regarding representation, slavery presented another potential impasse for the delegates. Students could discuss the merits of and the political obstacles to abolishing slavery and the slave trade at this moment in America's history.

Students should also know that in both Jefferson's *Summary View of the Rights of British Americans* and at the First and Second Continental Congresses, abolition of the slave trade was agreed upon as desirable once independence was achieved. Many state constitutions had already passed legislation discontinuing the legal importation of slaves. In fact, every state except Georgia had put limits on slavery and the slave trade by the time the Convention convened.

The initial drafts of the Constitution did not include any prohibitions on slavery. What was finally included in Article I, Section 9 was due to substantive argument and disagreement among the delegates, with the delegations from New Jersey, Pennsylvania, Virginia, and Delaware holding out for further restrictions on the slave trade and its eventual abolition. There were delegates that refused to sign the Constitution in part because it did not outlaw slavery or the slave trade.

What was included in the Constitution was the three-fifths clause that applied to all unfree persons, including black slaves; some black individuals were already free. This clause was not intended to exclude blacks from definitions of personhood; in fact, the designation of slaves as "persons" set a precedent for later arguments against those claiming that slaves were property. The three-fifths clause was not new to the convention, and Southern states would have been happy to have their slaves counted as full persons for the purpose of representation. This was objected to by Northerners: They argued that if slaves were to be counted as full persons for the purpose of representation, then possessions of Northerners should also be included in apportionment calculations. Thus, although Southern states were afforded greater representation as a result of this compromise, the apportionment also determined how much states would be taxed. This compromise benefited slave owning states while disincentivizing those states from obtaining more slaves.

The language addressing slavery made it clear that it was state laws that sanctioned slavery, not the Constitution.

ISSUES ADDRESSED AT THE GRAND CONVENTION: BILL OF RIGHTS

The absence of a Bill of Rights was an obstacle to only a few of the delegates, and it was assumed that such a bill would be added after ratification of the Constitution under the provisions of Article V for amendments to the Constitution. When the Constitution was presented to the states for ratification, New York refrained until assured that such a bill would be the first order of business for the new congress.

Teachers may want to discuss with students why the Convention delegates did not initially see a need for a Bill of Rights. Simply put, Madison and others believed that to list rights automatically precludes other rights, ones that may be overlooked in the process of writing such a bill. Furthermore, a bill of such rights in the Constitution has the potential to be seen as a grant of rights from the government rather than a recognition of prior, natural rights. Rights that are granted are rights than can be revoked.

RELIGION AT THE GRAND CONVENTION

A word or two on religion and the unique experience of the colonies is informative. Seventy to eighty percent of the population at the time of the convention was religious, and although the Founders did not share the same religious beliefs, they did share the conviction that religion was a powerful support for virtue and moral character, prerequisites to effective self-rule and ordered liberty. Thus, while they abhorred religious tests or qualifications for office, the Framers saw no contradiction in allowing government support for religious expression in a non-coercive manner.

Their religious convictions informed their commitments to the dignity of all human beings even while acknowledging man's tendency to corruption. On the one hand, because their Christianity informed them that all are fallen, they believed that no one could be trusted with absolute power. On the other hand, by virtue of the God-given capacity to reason, human beings are capable of self-government.

THE PREAMBLE TO THE CONSTITUTION

We recommend that the students memorize the Preamble as the teacher leads discussions on the elements of this statement of purpose for the proposed law of the land. Students should understand the stated purpose of this Constitution and that the function of a preamble to any law is to specify that purpose.

This preliminary discussion should highlight the nature of this Constitution as a limiting document—that is, as a document that limits the authority and, therefore, the power of the government established by the Constitution. These discussions will no doubt anticipate some of the provisions incorporated into the final document. Rather than discussing those at this juncture, teachers may want to flag them for further discussion when relevant sections of the constitution are studied. For example, students may discover the importance of dissent in a representative government and propose the right to free speech as a protection for meaningful dissent. Rather than discussing the First Amendment at this point, the teacher can recognize the insight and assure students that a return to the issue is forthcoming.

It is helpful to frequently remind students of the historical experience out of which the Constitution was written. Thus, we recommend a careful study of the colonial experience, including the War for Independence, prior to or in conjunction with a study of the Constitution. Whenever possible, the teacher should refer to the historical foundations of the principles embodied in the Constitution. For example, the teacher might ask why the delegates fear the power of a representative body. (They had experienced the coercive nature of a Parliament, unchecked by a king.)

We encourage teachers to lead discussions rather than give lectures; the students should be encouraged to enter a conversation, debating the issues with the experiences of the colonists in mind. The conversations at the Convention were at times scholarly, but the men in attendance were also immensely practical and, coming from different states, had varied concerns on their minds. The students should get a feel for this experience as they debate these issues. They will gain greater appreciation for the monumental task facing the representatives as well as for the beauty of the document those men wrote.

DISCUSSION QUESTIONS FOR THE PREAMBLE

Discussion of the Preamble and the Constitution proper should take approximately twenty hours of class time, including any lectures on the background provided above.

We recommend beginning this study by first reading the Preamble aloud. The following is a list of discussion questions, organized by element, to be considered:

We the People

1. What does the use of the word "people" imply? How is this different from the Articles of Confederation?

2. Who is included in the "we"? Are those who did not vote for ratification included in the "we"?

3. What principle from the Declaration does this element of the Preamble harken back to?

4. Who is the final arbiter of government under this constitution?

Establish Justice

1. If constitutional government is by nature just—because it is dependent upon consent of the governed—to what does this "justice" refer? Equality? Fairness? In other words, why include this provision in the Preamble if the entire Constitution establishes justice?

2. What is the principle of majority rule? Can majorities be unjust?

3. What if courts, the arbiters of justice, are corrupt?

Insure Domestic Tranquility

1. Why is the effort to ensure civil peace so important to society? What are the consequences of civil discord?

2. What about dissent? How is it to be expressed under a constitution that guarantees "domestic tranquility?"

3. Does ensuring domestic tranquility potentially interfere with our civil liberties? How so? Should it interfere? Are there any lines that should not be crossed? What are they? Can we cite any historical examples?

Provide for the Common Defense

1. How is this provision different from the other principles of the Preamble?

2. The costs and the extent of our present defense needs could be discussed. Is this what the Framers envisioned?

3. What are the dangers associated with this provision? What are the protections against a standing army afforded to citizens by the Constitution? (See later Article I, Sections 8 & 10; Article II, Section 2; Article III, Section 3.)

Promote the General Welfare

1. What does the word "welfare" mean? Does the addition of "general" change our understanding? Is our current understanding of welfare the same as the Framers' understanding? Is there any way to tell from the Constitution itself? Note that in Section 8 of Article I, "welfare" is again used. Do the two references to welfare refer to the same thing?

2. What is the role of government in securing the welfare of its citizens? Why would the Framers believe that promoting citizens' welfare should be included as a purpose of the Constitution? Does this principle have any connection to the Declaration of Independence?

Secure the Blessings of Liberty

1. What is liberty? Is it the same thing as freedom? What is political liberty? Can we be said to be free if we live under laws?

2. How does living under a constitutional government create the possibility for freedom? The colonists were under the British constitution. Were they free?

3. What if one's representative does not represent the views of his constituency in Congress? How do the Framers understand representation? Is representation in the Constitution purely democratic?

4. Discuss the following excerpt from Locke:

> [F]or law, in its true notion, is not so much the limitation as the direction of a free and intelligent agent to his proper interest, and prescribes no farther than is for the general good of those under that law: could they be happier without it, the law, as a useless thing, would of itself vanish; and that ill deserves the name of confinement which hedges us in only from bogs and precipices. So that, however it may be mistaken, the end of law is not to abolish or restrain, but to preserve and enlarge freedom: for in all the states of created beings capable of laws, where there is no law, there is no freedom: for liberty is, to be free from restraint and violence from others; which cannot be, where there is no law… (Second Treatise of Government, Chapter VI, Paragraph 57).

THE CONSTITUTION OF THE UNITED STATES

Students are now ready to turn their attention to reading the Constitution proper. Teachers may page through the document with the students to provide an overview: seven articles divided into sections and some sections further divided into clauses. It is helpful for students to know this terminology and how to use it when referring to the document.

It is advisable to take one article at a time with the students, reading and discussing each carefully. Teachers will need a good understanding of the debates over the various issues to guide students to a thorough understanding of the decisions embodied in the Constitution. For example, when discussing the bicameral legislature, the teacher should provide background by referencing the debates over representation and mixed government (see above).

Some questions require information about current affairs. Students should be encouraged to seek this information from newspapers or reputable online sources. Teachers will also need to provide some historical information that is not contained in the document itself. For example, it was Franklin Roosevelt who expanded the number of cabinet members.

Also included in this guide are references to diagrams and slides that can be found on the internet (see Appendix A: Online Sources). These aids help to summarize and visualize the Constitutional principles outlined in each article.

DISCUSSION QUESTIONS FOR THE CONSTITUTION

Article I— Legislative

1. Why does the first article of the Constitution focus on the legislative branch? What principle does this support? Why not the executive branch? To whom does the legislative branch answer most directly?

2. What is the fundamental responsibility of the legislative branch?

3. How is the legislative branch divided? Why? What is the name given to this kind of legislative body? Referred to as a whole, what is the legislative branch called?

4. To what does the 3/5 compromise refer? Explain. What problem was it intended to solve?

5. How many members does the House have? What are the members called? How are the members apportioned? What is the membership based on? How is this apportionment assessed and changed and how often? How many citizens does one member of the House represent today? Which state received the most members in the first session of the House? How many members of the House were present at the first meeting? How many are there today as a fixed number? What happens if the population of a district changes? How long do members in the House serve? What is the title given to the member who runs the business of the House? Name your representative.

6. How many members of the Senate were present at the first meeting? How many members does it have today? What are the members called? How many senators does each state receive? How long do members serve? Why were the terms of the first senators shortened for two-thirds of those elected? How were members originally elected? How was this changed? What title is given to the member who runs the business of the Senate? Name your state's senators.

7. List the specific duties of both halves of the legislative branch.

8. List the qualifications for becoming a representative or senator. Why are the qualifications different for each office?

9. Which bills must be initiated in the House of Representatives. Why?

10. Explain the difference between a bill and a law. How does the one become the other?

(See Appendix A for diagram.) This is a long and complicated process. Why? What principle does this support?

11. When both chambers pass a bill, where is the bill sent? What three options are now available?

12. Explain each option and why the president might choose to do one over another.

13. How is a law passed without presidential approval? Why is this an important element of the law-making procedure? What principle does this secure?

14. If it is the legislative branch's responsibility to make law, can the president execute legislation he has authored? What is executive privilege?

15. Explain impeachment. Has anyone in the history of the United States been impeached? For what sorts of acts can a president be impeached? Which house handles impeachment and which handles the trial? Who presides over the trial?

16. What is the meaning of *habeas corpus*? Explain the historical reasons the Framers included this provision.

17. What is the meaning of ex *post facto*? Explain the historical reasons the Framers included this provision.

18. What is a *bill of attainder*? Explain the historical reasons the Framers included this provision.

19. What does it mean to say a power is *enumerated*? Where in the Constitution are the powers of Congress enumerated? What is the importance of enumerating powers?

20. What does it mean to speak of *implied powers*? Are they listed in the Constitution?

21. What are *concurrent powers*? Are they listed in the Constitution?

22. What is a *reserved power*? Where does the Constitution mention them?

23. Are any powers *prohibited* to the federal government? Are any powers *prohibited* to the states? Is it better to include or not include them in a written constitution? Explain.

24. Make a list of the *enumerated, concurrent, reserved, and prohibited powers*.

25. Explain these other legislative terms: pork-barrel legislation, log rolling, filibuster, cloture.

Article II—Executive

1. What authority does the executive branch have? What is the fundamental responsibility of the executive branch? In our current political experience, the chief executive office appears to be most important. Was this the Framers' intent? Explain.

2. How long is the presidential term of office? How many consecutive terms may a president serve? When and by what was this limited? What were the historical precedents for a two-term limitation? Who broke with this tradition?

3. When the president is dead, or otherwise incapacitated, who is next in line to fulfill the duties of the office? If that person is unable to fulfill the duties of the president, who are the next two officials in line?

4. Memorize the oath of office

5. President Washington established the tradition of appointing a cabinet of advisors to help him execute his duties. How many members were in the first cabinet? How many members are in the current cabinet? Why the change? Which president expanded the number of members to the presidential cabinet? Why?

6. Give the names of the following current cabinet members: Secretary of Defense, Secretary of State, Treasury Secretary, Attorney General (head of the Justice Department).

7. List three other cabinet positions and their current heads.

8. What is an agency? List some agencies. How are they different from cabinet offices? Are they under the direction of the executive office or the legislative office?

9. How is the President elected? Explain the electoral college as outlined in Amendment 12. Why did the Framers decide upon this method for electing the president? What principle does it support? What is the electoral college meant to be a guard against? (See Appendix A for diagram.)

10. Originally, how was the vice-presidential position filled? When and how did this procedure change?

11. What are the eight specific duties of the President?

12. Give examples of the executive branch at the state level. Give examples of the executive at the city level.

Article III—Judicial

1. What is the fundamental responsibility of the judicial branch?

2. How is the judicial branch organized? What is a circuit court?

3. What is the Supreme Court?

4. What cases are deliberated in federal courts?

5. What do *original jurisdiction* and *appellate jurisdiction* mean?

6. What constitutes treason according to the Constitution?

7. How many Supreme Court justices are there today? How many votes are required for a decision?

8. Who is the current Chief Justice?

9. For how long does a justice serve? Why did the Framers think it important to establish this length of service?

Article IV—States

1. What is dual citizenship? How do Americans have dual citizenship?

2. Article IV says that states must cooperate with one another in what? This provision was added to the Constitution for what purpose? Who does it refer to now?

3. What is the process by which a state becomes a state?

4. What three things does the federal government owe to the states?

Article V—Amendment

1. How are amendments proposed?

2. How are amendments ratified?

3. How many amendments have been added to the Constitution since its ratification? Discuss those you think are most important.

4. Why did the Founders intend it to be difficult to amend the Constitution? In what prior document was the sentiment expressed?

5. What may not be amended before 1808?

Article VI—Supreme Law

1. What does the second clause under Article Six mean?

2. What is the difference between oath and affirmation? Why was affirmation added to oath?

3. Who must, by oath or affirmation, support the Constitution?

4. What is said about religion? Why is this significant?

Article VII—Ratification

1. How many states were needed to ratify the Constitution making it the supreme law of the land?

2. How many states did ratify it? Which state was first to ratify? Which state was the last? What were some of the issues most hotly debated in the ratifying conventions? Pick one and explain how it was resolved if compromise was reached.

3. On what date was the Constitution signed?

4. On what date did it become the supreme law of the land?

This might be a good opportunity to write an essay. Please see possible essay questions at the close of this guide.

THE BILL OF RIGHTS—THE FIRST TEN AMENDMENTS

Discussion of the Bill of Rights should take approximately five hours of class time.

Students should understand the reasons a bill enumerating the rights of citizens was not originally included in the Constitution and how its necessity was argued for by George Mason and Thomas Jefferson, among others. The latter, it should be noted, was not present at the convention.

Madison opposed such an addition, arguing that to enumerate rights provided the opportunity for infringement upon those very rights because such enumeration would be understood by those seeking power through government as the *only* rights citizens possessed. By its very nature, a constitution, Madison claimed, limits government; to include a list of rights ran the risk of omitting some and might give the impression that rights are *granted* rather than *"insured"* by government. It is important for students to understand the difference. Madison became convinced of the need for these ten amendments only after much debate.

Depending on the abilities of the students, some discussion of rights may be necessary. It is important for students to understand the difference between a *right*, a *privilege*, a *power* and a *responsibility*. Reference to the inalienable rights mentioned in the Declaration is helpful here.

Furthermore, students should be reminded that the protections enshrined here are protections against the federal government: The guarantee, while extending to all citizens of the United States, specifies only what the federal government may not do. States may decide otherwise. For example, when discussing the amendments regarding trial proceedings, the rights of the accused, etc., it is federal courts that are directed, not state courts. With this understanding, students will better see the significance of the Fourteenth and Fifteenth Amendments.

Students should discuss each of the first eight amendments in the context of the War for Independence; each was a direct response to colonial experience prior to declaring and winning independence. This discussion will help alleviate confusions about what the Framers intended, and it will ground their understanding in historical events. Students should be reminded that a long tradition in English law and practice, dating back to the Magna Carta (1215), included protections for individual liberty. Although this is not a course in that legal tradition, students should be aware that the Framers were articulating rights and responsibilities that had a long history.

Teachers could review the Preamble with the students, relating each of these amendments to the six principles embodied there. The Ninth and Tenth Amendments grew out of the debate at the convention and the subsequent debates at the ratifying conventions. These two amendments were meant to secure the principles of federalism and consent of the governed as well as to protect infringements upon personal liberty.

The original Bill of Rights included twelve rights which were not all passed by the first Congress. The ten that we have were the result of further debate and compromise, as was the Constitution itself.

We again recommend the *Heritage Guide to the Constitution* for teachers needing background information. Each of these amendments is complicated, and each has been litigated several times before many courts. Students need not understand all of the background history—that would be to provide a course on Constitutional law and move well-beyond the scope of this guide. Teachers need only present a basic understanding with some discussion of the implications of each amendment.

We have included the following discussion questions and notes for the teacher for each of the first ten amendments. These are meant to guide discussion. They are not to be handed out to the students.

DISCUSSION QUESTIONS AND POSSIBLE CORRESPONDING RESPONSES

First Amendment—The Five Freedoms

1. What are the five freedoms listed in the first amendment?

2. Explain each of the freedoms.

3. Can you think of the historical precedents informing this amendment?

4. Which objective(s) of the Preamble are addressed by this amendment?

This amendment attempts to "insure the domestic tranquility" as promised in the Preamble by securing these five freedoms.

Freedom of Religion: The fourteenth through the seventeenth centuries saw the seemingly unending civil strife and violence of religious wars, which many of the settlers to America were fleeing. Religious freedom in the newly organized and politically free United States was uppermost in the minds of the Framers.

Students could read excerpts from Jefferson's *Letter to the Danbury Baptists* as well as the *Virginia Statute for Religious Freedom* penned in 1786. Madison's *Memorial and Remonstrance Against Religious Assessments* (1785) is also instructive. They should understand what is meant by the so-called "establishment clause": Government shall make no law that requires citizens to observe the religious beliefs and practices of any specific denomination. It was not the intention of the Framers to drive religion out of the public square. Indeed, as they may recall from their study of the colonial settlements, students will connect this amendment to those earlier struggles for religious freedom. The "free exercise" freedom. A discussion of recent cases regarding religious freedom can be instructive.

Freedom of Speech: Students should recall the Sons of Liberty and their attempts to promote liberty through the Committees of Correspondence. Those participating in discussions of liberty were considered traitors by Britain, and Paul Revere, Samuel Prescott, Richard Dawes and Samuel Adams, among others, had to hide in order to avoid arrest for their activities.

Freedom of the Press: It is worth considering what is meant by this freedom in the context of the digital age; an increased amount of information is available to anyone. Should there be parameters and checks on what can and cannot be said in the press? Current federal and state laws regarding "hate speech" could be considered and discussed.

Freedom of Assembly: Students should recall the overbearing presence of British soldiers and the quelling effect their presence had on the right to assemble.

Freedom of Petition: Students should recall the Olive Branch Petition and the right of British citizens to directly petition their king. They could also reread the Declaration of Independence as a list of petitions and grievances the colonists addressed to the king. Petitions are frequently circulated today. How effective are they?

Second Amendment—The Right to Bear Arms

1. What does this amendment mean? Why did the Framers think it necessary to include this right?

2. Is it still necessary to have this right ensured?

3. What does it mean to say that citizens hold this as a right?

In recent years, this amendment has come under scrutiny, challenged as no longer necessary. Again, placing it in historical context can help the students understand the thinking of the Framers. (See *Heritage Guide to the Constitution* for a fuller treatment of the following.)

Students will be familiar with the outbreak of hostilities at Lexington and Concord. Armaments were stored in a magazine for use by colonial militias when defense of the settlement against aggression from either Indian attacks or even other colonies was needed. In this sense, the magazine represented the citizens' armory and the right and responsibility of the citizens to defend themselves in militias. With the advent of a peacetime standing army authorized by the Constitution, the question emerges: Who is the potential enemy against which citizens may have to defend themselves? And who has the primary responsibility for engaging in that defense? Students should recall these pre-war events to answer these questions.

It was the colonial governments under the authority of King George III that posed the greatest threat to safety in the years leading up to the war. It was not only at Lexington and Concord that the king's army attempted to secure the armory for their own use; at Williamsburg and other locations, armories were seized by the representatives of the crown and were intended for use against the citizens of the colonies. The King sent British soldiers as well as mercenaries ostensibly to keep the peace, but their presence was sometimes violent and violently received. Furthermore, historical precedents reaching back to Julius Caesar warned against a standing army at the service of one ruler, especially in times of peace.

It is clear from the Constitutional debates that, from the Anti-Federalist position, a potential future enemy was the very government created and at the same time limited through a written constitution with checks and balances. On the one hand, lack of federal forces would leave the newly formed United States vulnerable to foreign invasion. On the other hand, it was argued that a federal force could be used for tyrannical purposes against the states. The decision to allow Congressional regulation of state militias was controversial as it threatened the principle of federalism by putting these state militias under the authority of the national government.

One check on this national authority was to require appropriations for the standing army to be revisited and renewed every two years. Further, although the president is commander-in-chief, he must obtain congressional approval for a declaration of war. These measures minimized the possibility of a presidential tyranny but did not prevent a tyrannical national government. Through the 1800s, the army continued as an extension of the states' militias with armies called for a specific purpose and disbanded when the threat was averted or defeated. The citizen militias could be supplemented as needed by part-time, occasionally trained men.

President Washington was granted the right to call together armies as time and circumstances required, and a War Department was expected to handle whatever emergencies might arise. When it was eventually seen as necessary to have a standing army during peacetime, trained and ready to be deployed, it was primarily understood as a defense against foreign invaders.

During the Cold War, the United States moved toward establishment of a large military during peacetime. But even with a large military establishment, it was still the draft that filled the ranks with citizen soldiers. With the end of the draft in 1973, the professional or career soldier replaced the model of citizen soldiers.

Although the military was frequently used as a policing force, by 1904 the army was returned to its original purpose. The tradition of "watchmen" and other law enforcement bodies dates to the earliest days of colonialism. By the 1840s, with increased immigration and subsequent population explosions in urban areas, policing became a necessity. However, police forces remained under the jurisdiction of local authorities.

Madison recognized the dangers of a federal army and wrote in *Federalist #46:*

> Besides the advantage of being armed, which the Americans possess over the people of almost every other nation, the existence of subordinate governments, to which the people are attached and by which the militia officers are appointed, forms a barrier against the enterprises of ambition, more insurmountable than any which a simple government of any form can admit of. Notwithstanding the military establishments in the several kingdoms of Europe, which are carried as far as the public resources will bear, the governments are afraid to trust the people with arms. And it is not certain that with this aid alone they would not be able to shake off their yokes.

The Constitution gives to the federal government nearly unobstructed military authority, but, at the same time, it guarantees the right to bear arms to the citizenry as one check on this authority. In other words, although the federal government, according to the Second Amendment, has no authority to infringe upon private citizens' rights to own firearms, Congress retains the power to regulate this ownership and use of firearms.

Third Amendment—Protection Against Quartering of Troops

1. To what practice does this amendment refer? What historical precedent(s) did the Framers have in mind?

2. Since contemporary military forces are not in need of housing by the public, does this amendment apply today?

Discussion of this amendment could include reference to the rights to privacy and private land ownership vs. the needs of the military to house its soldiers in specific areas of the country.

Fourth Amendment—Protection Against Unlawful Search & Seizure

1. What constitutes an unlawful search or seizure?

2. What constitutes a lawful search or seizure?

3. What historical precedent set the stage for this amendment?

4. What are the rights of a citizen with respect to the police?

5. Does this amendment establish a right to privacy? If so, how far does that right extend? What does a "reasonable expectation of privacy" cover?

6. What does "probable cause" mean?

7. How is this protection enforced today? Was that enforcement specified in the Constitution?

In 1761 James Otis argued on behalf of individuals prosecuted under the writs of assistance. Under these writs, royal representatives (usually customs agents) carried out what was considered by many colonists to be an illegal search and seizure of property. Although justified, perhaps, by the threat posed by rampant smuggling, royal officials searched anywhere for anything. During the years leading up to the Declaration of Independence, prominent men involved in discussions of independence were frequently investigated, their premises searched and papers seized.

Otis lost his case, but two other similar cases in Britain found for the defendant. Thus, the practice of holding government authorities responsible for illegal searches and seizures had legal precedent prior to the Convention. The questions before the court then and now are what constitutes a search or seizure and whether the search or seizure is reasonable. (See *Heritage Guide to the Constitution* for a fuller treatment of this background.)

Similarly, the warrant clause has a legal history beginning in Britain, where warrants were not required but recommended as a protection for the policing authority against damage suits. Today, warrants most often provide protection for citizens against intrusions by police upon the privacy of citizens. Warrants must specify what is to be searched and what the search is for. Furthermore, warrants are issued under oath by an officer of the judiciary, a provision not specified in the language of the amendment.

Most scholars agree this clause was meant to prevent the kind of general and sweeping searches that had occurred during the pre-war years. Most legal cases today are prosecuted on grounds of what counts as probable cause. A discussion of when, what and how police may search is worthwhile.

The original intent of these clauses is widely argued, and in the twentieth century, several cases made their way to the Supreme Court. While understanding these cases is helpful for the teacher, the students need not be introduced to them. However, discussions of what qualifies as a reasonable expectation of privacy and what the costs and benefits are to public safety are helpful in unpacking the impact of this amendment.

Amendments Five through Eight

Students usually have only a vague notion of how the justice system works; thus, a brief introduction to the system is helpful before discussing the next four amendments.

Most federal grand juries seat twenty-three citizens. Initial proceedings take place between this jury and the prosecutor only. The details of the case are kept in confidence by the prosecution and jury; the procedure is closed to the public, and only witnesses may disclose information. The prosecutor may recommend that the jury subpoena witnesses to testify on behalf of the prosecution. Once the jury has heard evidence against the accused, they deliberate and decide whether the prosecution has presented sufficient evidence for a formal indictment. The accused must then be tried and the accusations "proven beyond a reasonable doubt" for conviction.

Grand juries are intended as a protection against prosecutorial overreach. However, because of the closed nature of the proceedings, the accused have little protection against incomplete or false information being presented to the grand jury. The accused is not represented by a lawyer when evidence is presented to the grand jury, and the grand jury usually follows the counsel of the prosecutor. (See Heritage Guide to the Constitution for a fuller treatment of this background.)

The constitutional issues and historical precedents for these amendments are far reaching and complicated. Students need only provide basic answers to the following questions and will need help even for that.

Fifth Amendment—Rights of the Accused in Criminal Proceedings

1. What is a grand jury? What is the function of a grand jury?

2. What is the difference between criminal and civil cases?

3. What rights should an accused person be afforded?

4. What qualifies as sufficient evidence to bring a case to trial?

5. What constitutes "reasonable doubt"?

6. What does "twice put in jeopardy of life or limb" mean? Can a citizen be prosecuted in federal courts after a state trial or vice versa?

7. What are Miranda rights?

8. What is "due process"?

9. What does the practice of eminent domain entail?

Sixth Amendment—Rights of the Accused, continued

1. What are the historical circumstances that placed this right foremost in the Framers' minds?

2. What constitutes a "speedy" trial?

3. How long does the process from indictment through verdict and sentencing normally take?

4. Are criminal trials open to the public? Why is this important? Under what kinds of circumstances might a trial be closed to the public?

5. Explain what trial by jury means.

6. Must the decision of a jury be unanimous?

7. Are defendants guaranteed a right to counsel at public expense?

The right to a speedy and public trial dates to the response by Sir Edward Coke in 1642 to the crown's practice of placing enemies in the Tower of London without trial and to the pre-Glorious Revolution practices of the Star Chamber. To prevent these abuses, the Constitution guarantees the rights of habeas corpus, to non-excessive bail, and to a speedy, public trial.

Another important protection provided by the Sixth Amendment dates to the twelfth century Constitutions of Clarendon and to the Magna Carta of 1215: the right to know of what one has been accused. The Framers, aware of the dangers of endless questioning by officials without specific charges made, included this protection as well as the right to "be confronted with the witnesses against him," that is to know by whom he has been accused.

Seventh Amendment—Rights in a Civil Suit

The historical background for this amendment is much more complicated than may be apparent. Students need not know all the details from debates at the Grand Convention, nor need they understand the arguments of the Anti-Federalists. However, they should recall that in 1775, and again as part of the complaints listed in the Declaration of Independence, colonists opposed the extension of royal courts over colonial matters because they did not provide a jury of one's peers.

Eighth Amendment—Punishments

1. What constitutes excessive bail?

2. What constitutes "cruel and unusual punishment"? What about capital punishment?

3. Are there cases in which no bail should be allowed?

Students should understand that the answer to these questions is largely a matter for the legislative branch. This is a check on the arbitrary and political use of power by the executive or judicial branches. For example, it is a matter for law to determine the punishments and fines for specific breaches of law. It was thought unlikely that the legislative branch, as representatives of and answering to the citizenry, would assign excessively severe punishments.

Teachers may want to discuss with the students the concepts of proportionality, deterrence, and Justice Warren's "evolving standards of decency." Students may find it informative to know the rulings of the Supreme Court on issues involving this clause.

Ninth Amendment—Powers Reserved to the People

1. What is the historical context for this amendment?

2. What is the purpose of a bill of rights?

3. Is there a danger in publishing a bill of rights that outlines specific rights?

4. Is there a conflict between this amendment and the "necessary and proper" clause? Explain.

To understand the importance of this amendment to the first Congress, students should revisit the concerns of Madison and others who opposed inclusion of a bill of rights in the original Constitution. In brief, they feared that an inclusion of rights would communicate that these rights were granted by the federal government to citizens as privileges; and, as privileges, they could be taken away by the federal government. The argument rests upon the principle that "the inclusion of one thing necessarily excludes all others." They further argued that the best protection of citizens' rights was a limitation on the powers of the federal government, i.e., the checks and balances embedded in the structure of the Constitution.

The Anti-Federalists disagreed, pointing to other rights already present in the Constitution, for example habeas corpus. The Constitution was ratified with an understanding that a bill securing individual liberties would be added by the first Congress.

This amendment was the closest thing to a compromise between those who saw the necessity of a bill of rights and those who saw such a bill as a dangerous precedent. The Ninth Amendment is meant to protect the rights of citizens against potential invasion of rights by the federal government. (See Heritage Guide to the Constitution for a fuller treatment of this amendment.)

Tenth Amendment—Powers Reserved to the States

1. The people are mentioned again here. How is this different from the Ninth Amendment?

2. What is the difference between a right and a power?

3. In what way does this amendment articulate the purpose of the entire Constitution?

4. Is there a conflict between this amendment and the "necessary and proper" clause? Explain.

Discussion of the Tenth Amendment provides the opportunity to look again at the purpose of the Constitution: to establish a limited and federal government. As with the Ninth Amendment, concern focused on whether a statement reserving power to the states would imply that the federal government possessed powers not yet enumerated or reserved to the states. If the Constitution did not grant power to Congress to interfere with individual liberty or state statutes, for example, it was argued that there was no further need to restrain the powers of the federal government through the addition of an amendment. However, the fear that federal government would overstep its constitutionally enumerated powers was strong enough to give voice to the reserved powers guaranteed by the Tenth Amendment.

Other Amendments

Students should know how many amendments have been made to the Constitution, noting that currently there have only been twenty-seven amendments passed—seventeen, not counting the original ten—in the two hundred plus years of the republic. It is interesting to note the years in which specific amendments were added.

Teachers may choose from the other seventeen amendments. In addressing these other amendments, we do not include discussion questions; the focus is on giving the students information. We suggest covering the following amendments and have included some minimal historical information:

Thirteenth Amendment—Abolition of Slavery

Teachers may decide to address the Thirteenth, Fourteenth and Fifteenth Amendments in the context of the Civil War. If studied as part of a unit on the Constitution, some background should be provided for the students.

While the Emancipation Proclamation delivered by Abraham Lincoln freed slaves as of January 1, 1863, that proclamation applied to the slaves living in the rebellious seceded states. Because they were in rebellion, states' rights would not be protected by federal law. After crucial victories by the North, Lincoln believed the time had come to issue this proclamation that abolitionists had long been advocating. There were, however, elements in the North opposed to emancipation; this proclamation freeing slaves in the rebellious South was a middle-ground position. Thus, the Emancipation Proclamation did not abolish slavery throughout the states.

Following the defeat of the South, a constitutional amendment would be required to abolish slavery throughout the Union. Proposed by Congress on January 31, 1865, the Thirteenth Amendment was finally ratified on December 6, 1865.

Although the Constitution places limits on the federal government, students should understand that the Thirteenth Amendment limits individual citizens as well as states. Neither has the liberty to own another human being.

Fourteenth Amendment—Definition of Citizenship

As with the Thirteenth Amendment, some historical context is helpful. When the Constitution was ratified, citizens of the several states were incorporated into the Union. Sixty odd years later in the Dred Scott v. Sanford (1857) decision, Justice Taney, writing for the majority, stated that "no black of African descent" could be considered and thereby protected as a citizen of the United States. This applied to both freemen and slaves. Passage of the Thirteenth Amendment moved several of the newly established Southern state governments to issue Black Codes, which, in practice, placed freed slaves back into near-slavery conditions by relegating them to a subordinate legal position. In response, Congress passed the 1866 Civil Rights Act. However, it was not clear that Congress was constitutionally empowered to pass such legislation. Thus, the 1868 passage of the Fourteenth Amendment reinforced protections against state actions that prevented full participation in citizenship rights. The rights of citizenship could not be prevented by any state; the newly freed slaves were to be recognized as citizens of the United States and of their state of residence.

Even with the requirement that seceded states ratify the Fourteenth Amendment before reincorporation, controversy and disagreement would continue: among other considerations, the use of public and private services and spaces, and the authority of the federal government to enforce federal laws upon the states, would be the subject of much debate.

The Equal Protection Clause, originally meant as a protection for freed slaves, became the subject of debate for all recognized protected classes. At the time of its passage and in subsequent years, what equal protection included was debated. It was only after the election of 1866 and the victory of the Republican party that the Fifteenth Amendment, extending voting rights to all citizens, was written and ratified.

The Enforcement Clause as part of the Fourteenth Amendment grants Congress the power to legislate enforcement of this amendment. In this way, the Enforcement Clause resembles the Necessary and Proper Clause of Article I, Section 8 of the Constitution.

Students should understand that the power of Congress to enforce the provisions of the Fourteenth Amendment through legislation refers only to state actions, not to actions taken by private citizens.

A person born "in the United States, and subject to the jurisdiction thereof" is regarded as a citizen under the Fourteenth Amendment. However, there is debate as to what qualifies as "jurisdiction." For example, do children born of illegal immigrants automatically become citizens? Although it is common to assume that such children are considered citizens under the language of the Fourteenth Amendment, the courts have not yet made that determination. (See Heritage Guide to the Constitution for a fuller treatment of this issue.)

The clauses dealing with representative apportionment, disqualification from public office, and payment of debt incurred by states in rebellion, are of primarily historical importance and are not addressed in this study of the Constitution.

Fifteenth Amendment—Suffrage Extended to All Races

On March 3, 1869, Congress approved the third of the Reconstruction Amendments. Again, teachers should place it in the context of that history. For example, it is worth noting that the Reconstruction Act of 1867, while granting suffrage to blacks in the South, did not require acceptance of this right in the North. Between the years 1865-1869, the number of those in favor of protecting black suffrage in the South and the North grew. This amendment's limited focus on race left open the possibility of discrimination based upon other standards; for example, literacy tests established in most Southern states effectively and disproportionately prevented many blacks from exercising the right to vote. This and other practices have been the subject of subsequent court cases.

Sixteenth Amendment—Establishment of an Income Tax

Students should understand that a tax on income was not part of the original Constitution. Ratified in 1913, the Sixteenth Amendment expanded Congressional authority to tax. Prior to ratification, taxation by the federal government was hindered by Article I, Section 2, Clause 3 and Article I, Section 9, Clause 4. In those Constitutional provisions, Congress could directly tax, but the share of the tax burden was to be divided between the states based on population. However, a state's high population may not translate into greater wealth. Members of Congress were thus hesitant to approve proposed taxation.

Seventeenth Amendment—Election of Senators by Popular Vote

Students should recall that in Article I, the Constitution provides for the election of Senators through state legislatures. Progressives, desiring to make the Constitution more democratic, insisted upon the need for direct election of senators. Thus, in 1913 the Seventeenth Amendment was ratified. It is important for students to recall the intent of the original practice: The Framers were thereby protecting federalism. Each senator, beholden to the legislature of his state for re-election, would be wary of approving federal intrusions upon the rights of his state.

Nineteenth Amendment—Suffrage Extended to Women

Even before ratification of the Nineteenth Amendment in 1920, many states had allowed women to vote. The Constitution itself never specifies that only men be given this right; thus, no amendment to this effect was strictly necessary for federal elections. Students may need to be reminded that, as was the case for the enfranchisement of blacks, states were within their Constitutional rights when setting qualifying standards for state elections. With the ratification of the Constitution, New Jersey allowed women to vote in federal elections, and in 1890 Wyoming followed suit. When the Nineteenth Amendment was ratified in 1920, thirty states had extended suffrage to women in most election processes. The Nineteenth Amendment, then, simply protects the right of women to vote in every state, thereby challenging Article I, Section 2 and Article II, Section 1, which left voting requirements up to the states.

BROADER QUESTIONS SUITABLE FOR ESSAY ASSIGNMENTS OR FURTHER DISCUSSION

1. How might the following three provisions of the Constitution create problems? Can these problems be resolved? How?

- Supremacy Clause
- Necessary and Proper Clause
- Tenth Amendment

2. What were three main issues debated at the Grand Convention? (See historical context above.) How was each resolved in this Constitution?

3. Define national, federal, and confederated government. Which did the Constitution establish? Why?

4. What is the difference between a democracy and a republic? Some scholars have argued that the U.S. Constitution established a democratic-republic. What do you think? Explain.

5. Discussion only: Summarize the three branches of government established by the Constitution. Draw a chart illustrating the checks and balances. What does checks and balances mean? Specifically, how does it work in this Constitution? (See Appendix A for two helpful diagrams.)

6. Is this a perfect constitution? Did the Framers believe they had written a perfect constitution? What is the evidence for your answer?

7. Recall the objections of the Anti-Federalists. Do you think the objections are well-founded? Why or why not? Pick one objection that you think is addressed in the final Constitution and explain how it is addressed.

8. What were the compromises reached on the issue of slavery? Were they adequate? Why or why not?

9. Why did some of the Framers consider a bill of rights a necessity and others consider a bill of rights dangerous? Be specific.

10. Since the temptations to power are not by any means eradicated by this constitution, how can the constitution be reasonably maintained? Did the Framers provide any constitutional barriers to the individual quest for power?

11. How is the making of the United States Constitution a historical anomaly? How is it different from anything that had preceded it?

APPENDIX A: ONLINE SOURCES

Numerous visual aids are available on the internet. These are a few recommendations.

Bill to Law:

https://thumbnails-visually.netdna-ssl.com/how-does-a-bill-become-a-law_50290b41c9938_w1500.jpg

Citizenship Practice Test:

https://my.uscis.gov/en/prep/test/civics/new

Checks and Balances:

https://21stcenturylearning.sharepoint.com/siteimages/checks%20and%20balances.jpg

http://www.kminot.com/art/charts/branches.jpg

Constitution:

https://www.heritage.org/constitution/#!/

Electoral College:

https://www.studentnewsdaily.com/wp-content/uploads/2016/11/Electoral-College_2016-820x477.jpg

Powers of each Branch:

https://image.slidesharecdn.com/seperationofpowers-checksandbalancesppt-121020150858-phpapp02/95/seperationof-powers-checksandbalancesppt-3-638.jpg?cb=1350745789

Miscellaneous and Documents:

http://www.constitution.org/primarysources/primarysources.html

https://www.archivesfoundation.org

http://teachingamericanhistory.org

APPENDIX B: LIST OF DOCUMENTS ARRANGED BY TOPIC[8]

On Independence

- *The Rights of British Colonies Asserted and Proved*, James Otis
- *Letters from a Pennsylvania Farmer,* John Dickinson
- *The Farmer Refuted*, Alexander Hamilton
- *Summary View of the Rights of British Americans,* Thomas Jefferson
- *Common Sense*, excerpts, Thomas Paine
- *On American Taxation*, Edmund Burke

On Size of the Republic

- *Federalist Papers,* Nos. 10, 14, 15, 23, 51
- *Federal vs. Consolidated Government*, Brutus
- *Argument against extended republic*, Centinel

On Federalism & Representation

- *Federalist,* Nos. 1, 6, 9, 10
- *Federalist,* Nos. 23, 39, 44, 45, 46
- *Federalist,* No. 39 On Separation of Power
- *Federalist,* Nos. 47, 48, 49, 50, 51

On the Legislature

- *Federalist*, Nos. 55, 57, 62, 63

On the Executive

- *Federalist*, Nos. 70, 71, 73

On the Supreme Court

- *Federalist*, No. 78
- *Marbury v. Madison*
- *The Problem of Judicial Review*, Brutus

On Religion

- *Letter to the Danbury Baptists*, Thomas Jefferson
- *The Virginia Act for Establishing Religious Freedom,* Thomas Jefferson
- *On Liberty,* John Winthrop
- *Memorial and Remonstrance against Religious Assessments*, James Madison

---

[8] Adapted from http://press-pubs.uchicago.edu/founders.

On Slavery

- *Federalist*, No. 54
- *Northwest Ordinance of 1787*

On National Security

- *Farewell Address,* George Washington

APPENDIX C: LIST OF IMPORTANT EVENTS LEADING TO THE CONSTITUTION[9]

Sugar Act of April 1764

Stamp Act of March 1765

Stamp Act Congress of October 1765

Declaratory Act of March 1766

Townshend Act 1767-1768

Boston Massacre of March 1770

Establishment of Committees of Correspondence in March 1773

Tea Act of May 10, 1773

Boston Tea Party in December 1773

Intolerable Acts/Coercive Acts 1774

First Continental Congress & adoption of Suffolk Resolves in September 1774

Lexington & Concord on April 19th, 1775

Second Continental Congress in May of 1775

Common Sense published in January of 1776

Declaration of Independence passed on July 4th, 1776

Articles of Confederation final draft submitted to the states in November 1777 with final ratification on March 1, 1781

Saratoga, October 1777

Valley Forge, winter of 1777-1778

Pennsylvania regiment mutiny January 1st, 1781

Siege of Yorktown, September 28 through October 19, 1781

Cornwallis surrenders at Yorktown on October 19th, 1781

Treaty of Paris signed September 3rd, 1783; ratified by Congress in 1784
Annapolis Convention in September of 1786

---

[9] Adapted from *Debate on the Constitution, Part One*, 1055-1099, Bernard Bailyn editor.

The Grand Convention of Philadelphia (later called the Constitutional Convention) convenes in May of 1787 and continues through September 17th

Constitution ratified by nine states necessary by June 21, 1788

Washington is elected first President and Congress writes Bill of Rights to be sent to the states for ratification in 1789

Bill of Rights ratified by Virginia, the eleventh state, and the first ten amendments are added to the Constitution in 1791

APPENDIX D: INTERESTING FACTS AND STATISTICS[10]

Colonial Americans were highly literate, a fact that helps us understand the high degree of civic participation and discussion (town halls and local governments).

In 1776, the population of the colonies was 2.5 million, 20% of the total population of England.

In 1790, population had nearly doubled to just under 4 million.

The largest city in the colonies was Philadelphia with 20,000 inhabitants, making it the logical meeting place for Congress and the Grand Convention. By way of comparison, London at the time had a population of 800,000.

Among the delegates at the convention, 37 of the 55 had attended college.

The average age of the delegates was 43, with Benjamin Franklin aged 81 and Jonathan Dayton the youngest at 26.

Twenty-one of the delegates had fought in the war and eight had signed the Declaration of Independence.

Seven of the delegates were or had been governors.

Neither Thomas Jefferson nor John Adams were present at the Convention. They were in France negotiating details of the treaty.

During the convention, Morris, Wilson, Sherman, and Madison—with his very soft voice—spoke most frequently and longest.

The Convention met in general meetings, Committees of the Whole, and divided up into Committees of Detail.

New Hampshire could not afford to send delegates to the Convention, but in late June John Langdon and Nicholas Gilman set out on their own dime. They arrived in late July, missing the major debates.

Rhode Island did not send delegates.

George Mason, Edmund Randolph and Elbridge Gerry voted against the Constitution and refused to sign.

---

[10] Adapted from Matthew Spalding, *We Still Hold These Truths*, 7-27.

BIBLIOGRAPHY

Adams, John. *The Political Writings of John Adams*, edited by George W. Carey, Regnery Publishing, Inc., 2000.

Adler, Mortimer. *We Hold These Truths: Understanding the Ideas and Ideals of the Constitution,* Macmillan, 1987.

Bailyn, Bernard. *Ideological Origins of the American Revolution*, Belknap Press, 1992.

Bailyn, Bernard. *Origins of American Politics*, Random House, 1968.

Bailyn, Bernard. *To Begin the World Anew: The Genius and Ambiguities of the American Founders*, Alfred A. Knopf, 2003.

Beitzinger, A.J. *A History of American Political Thought*, Dodd, Mead & Company, 1972.

Carey George W. *In Defense of the Constitution*, Liberty Fund, 1997.

Collier, Christopher & James Lincoln. *Decision in Philadelphia*, Ballantine Books, 1986.

Debate on the Constitution, Part One. Bernard Bailyn editor, The Library of America, 1993.

Drinker Brown, Catherine. *Miracle at Philadelphia, the Story of the Constitutional Convention, May to September, 1787*, Back Bay Books, 1986.

Flexner, James Thomas. *Washington, the Indispensable Man*, Back Bay Books, 1994.

Forte, David & Matthew Spalding. *The Heritage Guide to the Constitution*, Regnery Publishing, 2014. See also online resource at heritage.org.

Hamilton, Alexander, John Jay & James Madison, Edited by George W. Carey and James McClellan. *The Federalist*, Liberty Fund, 2001.

Hyneman, Charles S. and Donald S. Lutz. *American Political Writing during the Founding Era, Volume I, 1760-1805*, Liberty Press, 1983.

Ketcham, Ralph, editor. *The Anti-Federalist Papers and the Constitutional Convention Debates*, Signet, 2003.

Locke, John. *Second Treatise on Government,* Hackett Publishing Company, Inc. 1980.

Life magazine, July 1987 special issue on the Constitution.

Madison. *Elliot's Debates, Volume III, Notes of the Debates in the Federal Convention of 1787 reported by James Madison*, edited by James McClellan & M.E. Bradford, James River Press, 1989.

McCullough, David. *1776*, Simon & Schuster, 2005.

McCullough, David. *John Adams*, Simon & Schuster, 2002.

Miller, William Lee. *The Business of May Next, James Madison and the Founding*, University of Virginia Press, 1993.

National Review, May 17, 2010 special edition on the Constitution.

Spalding, Matthew. *We Still Hold These Truths: Rediscovering Our Principles, Reclaiming Our Future*, ISI Books, 2009.

Walker, Graham. *Moral Foundations of Constitutional Thought*, Princeton University Press, 1990.